I0155622

EVEN ME

A Christmas Play For Your Sunday School

BY

KATHLEEN MORRIS

Rouge Publishing

Copyright Kathleen Morris 2013

978-1-927828-22-9

This book is a work of fiction. Names, characters, places, and incidences are the product of the author's imagination or are used fictitiously. Any resemblance to actual events, locals, or person, living or dead, is coincidental.

Copyright 2013 Kathleen Morris

All rights reserved. No part of this publication may be reproduced, distributed, or transmitted in any form or by any means, or stored in a database or retrieval system, without permission of the publisher.

Rouge Publishing

ISBN 978-1-927828-22-9

OTHER BOOKS BY KATHLEEN MORRIS

<u>Deep Bay Series</u>
Deep Bay Vengeance
Deep Bay Relic
Deep Bay Legacy (Coming 2014)
<u>Blood War Series</u>
The Prion Attachment
Blood Purge (Coming 2014)
<u>Short Inspirations Series</u>
Size Seven Shorts
Short End Of The Stick
Shortcut To Alaska
<u>Short Stories</u>
Along The Way - 12 Short Stories You Can
Read Along The Way
<u>Plays</u>
Time Will Tell - An Easter Play
Even Me - A Christmas Play For Your
Sunday School
All I Need Is Love - A Play For Teens
Lost And Found - A Children's Christmas
Play
Gotta Love It - A Humorous Play About
Rural Life

How - To Books
How To Make Eye Catching Ebook Covers Easily

Available on Amazon.com

DEDICATION

This play is dedicated to Mocha, and all those who have been told they're ugly, or feel unwanted, or become victims of those who think they're better. God loves you just the same! So don't let the bullies win!

TABLE OF CONTENTS

EVEN ME

A musical play for your entire Sunday school.

"EVEN ME" is a story about a skunk who is made to feel unwanted in the manger where Christ is born. The story is an allegory with a message so powerful it will help young and old understand that Jesus loves everybody no matter what. Narrated throughout, it is set up for a very large cast from preschool to teens. The musical works for your entire Sunday school. As a musical it consists of many easy song choices and one unique solo for the skunk, written by Kathleen Morris.

SCENE ONE

The scene has one opening set and remains through the entire play. It takes place in a shabby stable in Bethlehem. The animals are the main characters in the first half of the play while the shepherds are the main characters in the second half of the play. The story is about the Nativity but it takes on a different perspective from your average Christmas play. It is from the perspective of the animals and others who enter the stable. The main focus of the story is not just the actual birth of Christ but rather the message that the animals and the shepherds learn. They find out that Jesus has enough love for all of them and he loves them no matter what they look like, act like, or dressed like. They ultimately find out that Jesus' love is unconditional.

CHARACTERS

Narrator –
Is responsible to narrate the entire play.

Primary class animals –
Dressed as whatever animals they like.

Junior bug class –
Dressed as whatever kind of bugs they want.

Preteen girl cats –
Dressed as cats.

Preteen boy rats –
Dressed as rats.

Messenger angel –
Dressed as angel.

Music angel –

In charge of playing the violin or other instrument for various songs. There are no speaking parts. This is her only responsibility in the play. *(She dresses as angel)*

Snobby cat –

Dresses as cat, but has three lines in the play. Also plays her violin.

Ricki rat –

Dresses as rat but has one line.

Crow –

Dresses as Crow. Has loud voice. Known for her big mouth. She has two lines and must sing a solo.

Tuff cat –

Dresses as a cat, and has one line.

Skunk –

Dresses as skunk. She is shy. She has two lines in the play, and she must sing a solo.

Cool cat –

Dresses as a cat and has one line.

Ruff rat –

Dresses as rat and has one line in the play.

Ladybug –

She is shy. She dresses as a ladybug. She has one line in the play. She also plays her guitar.

Big bug –

He dresses like a bug and has one line in the play.

Mary –

She is dressed to fit her character. She has two lines in the play. She must sing a solo.

Joseph –

He is dressed to fit his character and has one line in the play.

Shep –

He is a loudmouth, rich shepherd. He is very proud. He has several lines in the play.

Moby –

He is Shep's dimwitted friend.

Spare shepherd –

They have no speaking parts, but are dressed as shepherds. They are teen boys.

Singing angels –

They are teen girls dressed as angels and sing "Emmanuel".

Three Kings –

Three teen guys dressed as kings. No speaking parts.

OPENING SCENE

Narrator –

It was a night like never before in a little town called Bethlehem. Above, in the eastern sky, a brilliant star illuminated the town with its brightness. A calm settled over the land, and over a little stable; the smallest, shabbiest stable in all of Bethlehem. The roof was leaking and the walls were falling apart. It was a place that most would not venture in. The stable was full of creatures of all kinds. They had just eaten their supper meal and were settling down for an evening of usual entertainment…and on this particular night, everyone seemed to be restless.

(Music starts – Out come the primary class animals. They can be various different animals. They do a special number to music.)

Narrator –

The baby animals were the cutest in the stable. All their parents were so proud. But they had to make way for the bugs, for they too lived in the stable, and wanted to do a special number.

(Music starts – Out come the bugs. The junior class. They do their performance and say a poem.)

Bugs –

We are the bugs;

The itty bitty bugs.

We crawl on our bellies;

And we live with the slugs.

We sneak right up;

And were very very quiet. (whisper)

We don't make trouble;

No…we wouldn't even try it!

Narrator –

The bugs loved to live in the stable. But they were very shy so they scurried away quite quickly. They didn't want to be stepped on by the cats anyway.

(Music starts – Out come the cats. (Preteen girls class) they scurry around looking for rats and mice. They say their poem.)

Cats –

We're the cool cool cats
Of the stable here,
We feast on the mice
And the rat so near;
We dine on the milk,
And we lick our fur;
We're the best of the best,
And we purr, purr, purr! (make purring sounds)

Narrator –

The cats were naturally arrogant. They seemed to control most of the goings on in the stable. They demanded attention from the stable hands and became spoiled. Even the cows detested them when they stole their milk. There was only one animal that stood up to the cats, and that was the rat. In fact, there was an ongoing feud that lingered in the stable between the two of them. One always tried to out-do the other.

(Music starts –Out come the rats. (The preteen boys class) They stomp and flex their muscles to the music. They say a poem.)

Rats –

We are the rats, and were lean and mean;

We live in the barn and were seldom seen.

We're smart and sneaky and we might bite too;

So don't hurt us and we won't hurt you! (Act mean)

Narrator –

The cats became furious after what they heard the rats say. Their jealousy consumed them as they chased the cats in rage.

(Fast music is played – Cats chase and fight rats)
(All of a sudden, the fighting is interrupted by a loud bang as lights go out)

Narrator –

Suddenly…all goes dark…*(Lights out)*
The cats stopped chasing the rats, and the rats stopped fighting the cats. The cows went silent and the pigs didn't make an oink. Silence fell over the animals as a single star shone over an angel that started to speak.

Messenger angel –

Behold…I bring you good news. Tonight in this stable, a king will be born. His name will be Jesus. He has come to save you. So prepare for 'love' to come.

Narrator –

The animals jumped and howled with excitement. They couldn't believe that a king could be born in their stable; The lowliest, shabbiest stable of all. They hurried and straightened every inch of the stable. They fluffed the hay and cleaned up their stalls; they groomed themselves and even made a little manger bed for the king. They were so proud to have Jesus grace them with his presence. They began to discuss the details of his arrival.

Snobby cat –

I think Jesus will love me best. I'm purrrrfect!

Ricki Rat –

Yeah right! Everyone knows that rats are superior!

Narrator –

And with that, the feud was on-again, in spite of their expected royal visitor. They clawed and they hissed, and not only them, soon the whole stable was involved in an all out brawl. *(Animals fight while fast music is played)*

Narrator –

Suddenly...*(As music stops and whistle blows)*...without warning. The Crow, known for her big mouth, let out a most stupendous sound.

Crow –

STOP IT! STOP IT! STOP IT! Were going to scare Jesus away for sure...Then how can he love ANY OF US?

(Everyone yells and heckles at the Crow)

Tuff cat –

No... the crow's right... let her talk... If I don't eat her first *(Crow flinches)*

Crow –

Thank you cat... I think. Anyway, as I was going to say: Jesus can love all of us the same... so let's not fight.

Narrator –

As the Crow calmed them down, things started to get back to normal again. There was no more fighting amongst the animals. For they now all believed they would be loved by the King when he came. The cats gathered together and started to search for a perfect gift for Jesus. The rats gathered together and started to discuss what kind of gift they would give him as well. Even the bugs made a few plans of their own. The other animals quietly lay in expectation of what was yet to come. Strangely enough however…a very bad smell began to fill the stable.

Rude rat –

PEEEEEEEEE-UUUUUUU...SKUNK ALERT! SKUNK ALERT!

(All the other animals started to hold their noses and say. "PEEEE-UUUU!")

Narrator –

A skunk that had just been passing by had overheard the news of Jesus' birth. She was curious. She wanted to see if she could get some of that love they were talking about too. But…she soon found out that she wasn't welcome.

(Everyone yells, "Go away skunk" over and over)

Skunk –
But…but I just wanted to see Jesus. I want some of his love too!

(Everyone roars with laughter)

Cool cat –
Jesus won't love YOU! You're just a smelly old skunk.

Snobby cat –
Yeah…and your fur doesn't even begin to compare with our royal feline fur.

(Everyone laughs)

Ruff rat –

Go away, we don't want you here…you stink! Jesus wouldn't even go near you anyway.

(Everyone heckles)

Narrator –

So…the skunk, terribly upset, shamefully crept to the corner and began to cry. She couldn't believe how foolish she had been. She actually thought Jesus would love someone like her…a bad smelling, poorly groomed skunk.

(Bugs gather around skunk)

Ladybug –

Don't cry skunk. You never mind what they say. They're wrong...Jesus WILL love you!

Big bug –

Yeah… If he can love snobby cats, and mean old rats…and slimy bugs like us…then he can love you too!

Skunk –

(Sniffling) Really? I don't know…

(Skunk solo – EVEN ME)
(Guitar chords Em, D, C)
Note: Sheet music included below lyrics in it's original raw form. You may need to add or delete notes as needed.

EVEN ME

(Verse 1)
They say he loves
someone like me;
But I don't know
just how that could be;
I'm not the best
you know that too;
I could pretend
but that wouldn't do.
(Chorus)
So here I stand,
I've yet to see,

How Jesus loves,
Even me!
Lord here I am, it's little me;
Will you please love even me,
Even me!
(Verse 2)
They laugh at me
when I don't fit in;
But when I try to
I never can win;
Always the loser
Never okay;
How can He love me
If they think this way?
(Back to Chorus)

EVEN ME

Lyrics and music
Written by:
Kathy Morris
2001

Piano

Verse 1: They say he lo — ves some — one like
Verse 2: They laugh at me When I don't fit

me but I don't know just how that
in but when I try to I ne - ver

could be I'm not the be — st you know
Can win Al — ways the lo - oser Ne - ver

that too I could pre — tend but that
OK - ay How can he love me If

would ——— n't do   So hear I   stand   I've yet

they think this way

to   see   How Je ——— sus loves   Ev ——— ven

me   Lord hear   I   am It's li——ttle me   will

you please   lo — ve   ev — en   me   e — ven   me

© Kathy Morris 2001

30

Narrator –

But when the cats heard the skunk singing, they gathered around her and picked on her even more. They laughed and pointed and held their noses…and their ears.

Snobby cat –

We heard your ugly singing. You think we want to listen to THAT? You hurt our purrrfect ears. CATS… COVER!

(She covers her ears motioning for all the other cats to do the same.)

Narrator –

So the cats in the stable began covering their ears. They did not want to listen to anything more about the skunk. They didn't want her and her stinky smell ruining their perfect reputation. After all, they had an image to uphold…especially since Jesus was coming. But instead…something else happened. With a burst of heavenly might, and nearby angel who had overheard everything, rushed into the stable and took away the cats hearing…because of their arrogance. The cats were devastated. They couldn't hear a thing. They dashed around, and spun about, and shook their heads indignantly. They didn't know what to do. They feared that Jesus would never love them now…their perfect image had been tarnished. The other animals in the stable were scared. They didn't want to be next so they didn't say a word… And that was a good thing because very close nearby, they could hear that someone was coming.

SCENE TWO

(At this point, two shepherds enter the stage)

Shep –
This is the place I think.

Moby –
Yeah… But there's nobody here.

Shep –
Not yet, but there will be. I always like to be a little early. Gives me time to fix my hair. *(Pulls out a comb and starts combing his hair in an arrogant way.)* You think Jesus will like my hair this way…or like that?

Moby –

I don't know. *(says without care)*

Shep –

You *never* know…that's your problem man. You're not all there in the head *(taps a finger to his head making fun of him)* You see…if you want to be at the top of the list with this new Messiah guy, you gotta have some brains like me…or at least look like you do… Like check this out dude. *(Pulls out a flashy shepherds robe from the bag he's carrying. Holds it up to show his friend and then puts it on. He opens the lapels with both hands and twirls around as he shows off.)* Brought it all the way from Jerusalem. Top of the line. Pretty cool hey?

Moby –

Yeah… I guess.

Shep –

You guess? I look great and you know it! Jesus will be smilin' at me for sure. *(He puffs out his chest.)*

Moby –

is that all you care about?… Yourself?

Shep –

No…but…first impressions ARE everything you know. Like I said… I want to make SURE Jesus loves me.

(Angel enters the stage)

Messenger angel –

HEAR YEE...HEAR YEE...THE KING DOESN'T LOVE LIKE THAT!

Shep –

(Looks the angel over) WHOA! Bet you come straight from heaven, don't you? Could you put in a good word for me? *(He goes on like he's counting inventory)*… I have my own sheep business, I'm very wealthy…and I have…*(The angel interrupts)*

Messenger angel –

STOP! I TOLD YOU, THE KING DOESN'T LOVE LIKE THAT!

Shep –

Yeah whatever. *(He says this fast because he's too self-absorbed to listen.)* Anyway, I gotta get going, I still have to wash my feet. Gotta look good ya know.

(The angel looks at Moby with a puzzled look on her face. Moby shrugs with his arms out as if to say that he doesn't know what's wrong with his friend. Angel exits after him.)

Narrator –

Finally, after hiding in the stable for a very long time, the animals come out. They thought the people would never leave. They stretched and yawned and fluffed up there fur and relaxed…but not for long. Suddenly…a trumpet sounded… Mary and Joseph were on their way to the stable. The animals perked their ears up, and realized this was the moment they were all waiting for. They quickly straightened up the stable again and made sure the baby bed was ready. They whispered amongst themselves and decided that a special song was in order. *(Anyone that plays an instrument can play silent night while the other animals sing.)*

SILENT NIGHT SONG – *sang and played as Mary and Joseph go up.*

Narrator –

As Mary and Joseph made themselves comfortable in the stable, the animals gathered around to greet them. Before they knew it, baby Jesus was born. The animals were overjoyed to see the King born right there in their home. They jumped, hopped, rolled, and kicked until they were dizzy. It was truly a perfect moment…one the animals and creatures of the stable would never forget. They were so excited that they scurried away to get the gifts they had made for Jesus.

Mary –

Oh Joseph, isn't he wonderful? He truly is holy. *(Mary is looking at the baby in the cradle.)*

Joseph –

Yes…and greater than all the kings in this land!

Mary –

GREAT ARE YOU LORD…MOST HOLY LORD! *(Mary picks baby Jesus up out of his cradle and holds him out to the audience while saying her line, then cradles him in her arms and sings a solo to him. Music is played by violin. Music can be any praise song.)*

Narrator –

The animals heard the lovely singing and gathered around the Christ child. They had never before felt such love, such joy, or such peace in their little home until now. The animals felt honoured that Jesus would even be born in their home, especially the crow. She was so moved by the presence of God that she could not contain herself. She had to open her mouth…and when she did, the most beautiful sound came out.

(Crow solo – *Sing any praise song or Christmas song)*

Narrator –

Far beyond the stable, three Kings and some shepherds had followed the great star to Bethlehem. They were weary and tired from traveling so far, but they now knew their journey had come to an end. They had finally found the Messiah. *(Music is played "We Three Kings". As the kings walk up the aisle, the shepherds follow. They enter the stage and bow before Jesus, give their gifts, then stand behind Mary and Joseph. Or kneel to one side)*

Narrator –

Shep and Moby, the two shepherds who arrived earlier, had now found themselves late. Shep was so embarrassed; he covered his head in shame as he walked to the stable with Moby.

Shep –

HOW COULD YOU LET ME BE SO LATE MOBY? *(Yelling and punching Moby in the arm)*

Moby –

OWWWWW! It's not my fault you took so long washing your feet. They didn't have to be THAT clean.

Shep –

YES THEY DO! *(Yelling through his teeth)* I TOLD YOU I WANTED TO MAKE A GOOD IMPRESSION. YOU NEVER LISTEN TO ME YOU...YOU...YOU... *(God takes Shep's voice away stopping anything from coming out of his mouth. He is mouthing the words now and grabbing his throat, but nothing is coming out.)*

Moby –

SHEP...SHEP! What's wrong?

Narrator –

But... Shep couldn't tell Moby what was wrong. He didn't know that the Lord had taken his voice because of his pride. So the two of them entered the stable and bowed before Jesus anyway. Shep could not impress the Messiah with his wealthy tales or clean appearance. In fact, nobody even noticed his top-of-the-line robe.

Shep looked around and suddenly realized there was something more going on here than he thought…and it wasn't about him. For the first time ever, Shep didn't think of himself. He was secretly grateful that he wasn't able to speak. For it wouldn't have mattered one way or the other.

Angels began to fill the stable with their heavenly light, as they stood wonder struck at God's sweet power and love that he brought to life through his only son. All the animals in the stable and every living creature great and small, could feel the love that Jesus had for them.

They finally realized…that it doesn't matter whether you're big or little, rich or poor, or even what color you are. It doesn't matter if your clothes are old and worn, or if you look funny. God doesn't care if you have an unpleasant odour. He doesn't love you more just because you think you're perfect, cool, tuff, or better than anyone else. He doesn't love you less because you think you're too bad or imperfect. He loves the blind, the deaf, the dumb, the weak, the strong, and everything in between. JESUS LOVES EVERYONE THE SAME...AND HE WANTS TO LOVE YOU TOO!

Just remember the creatures of the stable. If Christ's love is big enough for all of them...including the skunk, then surely his love is big enough for you. Oh yeah...and cats...Jesus loves you too, in spite of your arrogance. So... He'll give you your hearing back as long as you promise not to make fun of others just because they're different...and Shep... God wants to love you and people like you...with no strings attached. So...you can use your voice again and sing along with us.

(Everyone sings "Jesus Loves Me" All musicians can play along.)

Narrator –
And all the angels gathered together in heaven and on earth to celebrate that glorious night. The night that unconditional love was born. The night that would prove to change the world and all who live in it. For this tiny

babe, in all his excellence, was born to save us all. He is our hope, our strength, our King and Lord Messiah, Redeemer…Saviour… Christ Emmanuel!

(Angels gather with everyone to sing a final song together. You can choose any suitable Christmas Carol or praise song. Spotlight is directed at them. All other lights are off.)

(Everyone bows, then exits the stage.)

THE END

ABOUT THE AUTHOR

Award-winning author Kathleen Morris has written numerous articles, poetry, and short stories published in various Saskatchewan newspapers. Her poem *Refuge* is published in a book anthology titled *A Golden Morning*. She has written many plays and skits including her play titled *Gotta Love It*, winner of Dancing Sky Theatre's rural writing contest in 2001 where it was also performed by the theatre troupe in Meacham, Saskatchewan.

Deep Bay Vengeance is Kathleen's first novel followed by its sequel *Deep Bay Relic*. She also writes non-fiction inspirational books about funny stories from her own life. Her latest novel is called *The Prion*

Attachment, first book in the *Blood War Trilogy.* When she's not writing, she enjoys spending time with her husband Barry and their three grown children at her home in Saskatchewan, Canada. For more on Kathleen Morris please check out her Amazon Author page at Amazon.com

OTHER BOOKS BY KATHLEEN MORRIS

<u>Deep Bay Series</u>
Deep Bay Vengeance
Deep Bay Relic
Deep Bay Legacy (Coming 2014)
<u>Blood War Series</u>
The Prion Attachment
Blood Purge (Coming 2014)
<u>Short Inspirations Series</u>
Size Seven Shorts
Short End Of The Stick
Shortcut To Alaska
<u>Short Stories</u>
Along The Way - 12 Short Stories You Can
Read Along The Way
<u>Plays</u>
Time Will Tell - An Easter Play
Even Me - A Christmas Play For Your
Sunday School
All I Need Is Love - A Play For Teens
Lost And Found - A Children's Christmas
Play

Gotta Love It - A Humorous Play About
Rural Life
<u>How - To Books</u>
How To Make Eye Catching Ebook Covers
Easily

Available on Amazon.com

www.ingramcontent.com/pod-product-compliance
Lightning Source LLC
LaVergne TN
LVHW051818080426
835513LV00017B/2005